Let's Go to a Show

by Linda Gold
illustrated by Darcia Labrosse

HOUGHTON MIFFLIN

BOSTON

Printed in China

ISBN 10: 0-618-88629-X
ISBN 13: 978-0-618-88629-6

56789 0940 16 15 14 13 12
4500365496

It's time to perform.
These bees need to get in line.

2 How are the bees different?

The first one is tall.
The next one is short.

What is the next bee in line?

These ants can do flips.
They can do splits.

4   Are there more ants doing flips or splits?

The ants go on stage, next.
Hurry, get in line.

How do the ants line up?

The fireflies are next.
They are ready to go.

How are the fireflies lined up?

Bees, ants, and fireflies all in lines.
It's a beautiful show.

Dancing Line

Draw

1. Draw a pattern like the bees on page 3.
2. Show tall, short, tall, short, tall, short, tall.

Tell About Follow Directions Oral and Written

1. Tell about the bees on page 3.
2. Tell the pattern the bees are in.

Write

Write the words *tall* and *short*.